I0489339

52 KILLER MARKETING TIPS

Marketing demystified in 52 killer tips that
your competition is probably forgetting about.

SANDY HIBBARD

52 Killer Marketing Tips
Text Copyright © 2014 by Sandy Hibbard
All rights reserved

Independently published by
Lyric Marketing & Design, Inc.
LyricMarketing.com
info@lyricmarketing.com
214-208-3987
ISBN-13: 978-1497327696

52 Killer Marketing Tips is taken from the blog
www.LyricsMarketingTips.com written and published by Sandy
Hibbard, CEO and Creative Director.

WHAT DOES YOUR MARKETING SOUND LIKE?

In 2000, I had the opportunity to buy a small advertising agency from a dear friend of mine and made the leap of faith from a long and successful corporate career in marketing and communications into the world of "agency". I started with a nice but small client list and went to work, thirteen years later, here I am! I continue to direct this little company and my team who has proudly provided marketing and advertising services for the Dallas/Fort Worth, Texas area in everything from real estate to luxury home building to authors, musicians and artists, to small and medium size businesses and entrepreneurs.

This past year I decided to work on an online project "*52 Killer Marketing Tips*" by creating a blog and posting weekly marketing tips that I strongly believe in, practice, and encourage my clients to engage in. This is that book! After thirteen years in the agency business and over 15 years in corporate communications, I have seen that one of the biggest obstacles for my clients and business prospects is knowing what to do when it comes to marketing. They may have an idea, or even know the results they want, but have a challenge in creating a strategy to make it happen. That is when they come to me. My job is to help them tell their story and strategically reach their audience with their message.

Times have changed and business has certainly changed over the past 13 years. Now information and DIY'ers abound, and for those who have limited marketing budgets, it is easier to produce effective marketing than ever before. That is what this book is about. I wanted to share with my friends and clients, followers and prospects, ideas and strategies on marketing, that if properly implemented, will push you far ahead of your competition. With these 52 KILLER marketing tips, you can literally design and build a strategy that will make your marketing sing throughout the year.

Take the weekend and sit down to review these 52 Killer Marketing Tips. Choose three to five that you KNOW you can put together yourself in the next few months. Then choose three to five or more that you feel you can implement over the next 12 months. Use these selected tips to build your marketing strategy, making sure your message is reaching your target audience every week.

Here's to making your marketing sing.....all the way to bank!

THANK YOU . . .

A special "thank you" to my team - Sarah Sellers, Gabby Jones, and Scott Kennedy - for their passionate support of Lyric Marketing & Design, our projects and our clients.

I would not have been able to get these tips out this year without the help and inspiration, writing talent, and marketing expertise of Sarah – THANK YOU, YOU ROCK!

Thanks to my dear friend Kelli Geopfert for helping me with my grammar and spelling on this project! And to my friend Stephen and my sisters Leisa and Judith - thank you for your advice, encouragement, brainstorming time, and those extra "eyes"…Love you guys!

52 KILLER MARKETING TIPS
TABLE OF CONTENTS

LYRIC'S MARKETING TIP #1:
EMAIL LIVES ON!

To improve your email reputation and achieve better results this year, create segmented groups in your email campaigns. Tailor your email messages to the specific needs of your clients and target audience. There is no one-size-fits-all customer, so determine who your various segments of target customers are and target your message accordingly.

LYRIC'S MARKETING TIP #2:
GET RID OF THAT NASTY HABIT

You may have heard me tell the story about the Skanky Scrunchie....if so, remember to clean up your marketing ASAP. If you haven't, the gist is this: Don't let one nasty, poorly designed, badly worded, embarrassing photo, or ANYTHING that doesn't represent how fabulous you are, get out on the web, over mobile, or into the hands of your public! One bad element can ruin an otherwise great presentation. And remember, if it goes out via email, mobile, or on the web, it is there forever. Present your business and your service with class and precision, good taste, and eye-catching design!

LYRIC'S MARKETING TIP #3:
ARE YOU IN THE GAME?

At the beginning of the new year, everyone is scrambling and getting back into the game to start their business year off with a bang. Is your marketing in the works for the new year? Have you WRITTEN down what you plan to do? Do you have a strategy? Download a Free worksheet at the RESOURCES tab on www.LyricMarketing.com and get started! Remember, no one knows what you (or your business) are doing if you don't tell them.

LYRIC'S MARKETING TIP #4:
MARKET WITH A WELL-TOLD STORY

What is YOUR story? What is the passion behind your business? I want to challenge you this week to think about your story. What gets you out of bed in the mornings to do what you do? Why do you love it? Nothing resonates with people more than a well-told, compelling story, so please, tell us. Tell your customers. Tell your prospects. Draw them in with a well crafted story that shares your passion for your business. To give you an idea of how a feature story is written visit the Resources tab at www.Lyricmarketing.com and download an example PDF.

LYRIC'S MARKETING TIP #5:
LET'S MAKE MARKETING FUN AGAIN!

Plan a simple party or get-together at your home, a wine bar or bistro. Make it an EVENT on Facebook and promote it on your page, your profile, website, blog and all your social media networks. Call and invite your customers, friends, and people you WANT to be your clients. Make a happening and promote it through your online channels - everyone wants to have fun and you can share your story over a glass of good wine, hot coffee, or a cold beer in an intimate setting. And don't stop at one, you might want to make this a monthly ritual!

LYRIC'S MARKETING TIP #6:
CHOOSE YOUR IDEAL CLIENT

Who is your ideal client? Cruise through your networks and search for people you WANT to do business with, then friend them, or invite them to follow you. Try to add 10 people to your networks every week that you would like to know and then engage them in conversation. And NEVER forget about your past and present clients, make sure they are in your pipeline of information!

I found this on Jive Communications blog and thought it was appropriate to share on this post: "If you want to have greatness in your life, you have to surround yourself with great people. Choose your company wisely. Be relentless in surrounding yourself with people who bring out the best in you and your business. Your success in life depends on it.

LYRIC'S MARKETING TIP #7:
THE HUB OF THE WHEEL

It's time to start thinking about a blog as being the HUB of your marketing wheel. If you are a specialist in your field, sharing that information becomes an educational channel for your clients and target customers. Provide your audience with information they can use about your industry. If you are a Realtor, why not publish a blog that contains valuable and timely market information or tips for homeowners?

Every industry has specific information that is valuable to their customers. Write it down in the form of an article and publish it to a blog, then share it out over social media. This is a tested and successful formula for increasing traffic to your website and engaging your target audience. Have fun with it!

LYRIC'S MARKETING TIP #8:
SMILE FOR THE CAMERA

I always say "smile for the camera, or look stupid, it's your choice." Post your photos. Use your photos to tell your story. Publish photos of your company events, of you in action, of your clients, of helping others. Don't just publish them to Facebook, but put them on Instagram, Flickr, your blog, Twitter, LinkedIn, Smugmug, Pinterest, and any other photo media outlet that will help them be found online. Create specific albums of photos of particular events. As the old adage says "a picture is worth a thousand words", so, don't be shy - and smile!

LYRIC'S MARKETING TIP #9:
SAVE TIME WITH A STRATEGY

Scared of blowing all your time on the social media machine? You want to avoid wasted time when posting in social media and make the most of your efforts, right? Of course! Let me share a simple tip on handling your time, when setting your schedule for your social media posts, decide how much time you have to devote to this marketing activity and then divide your time into thirds:

1- Creation of the content you will share

2- Observation of your network by listening to what they say

3- Participation in other outlets - comment, share, guest blog

Set a day and a time in your schedule to handle your social media and stick to it. If you build it, they will come. Download my FREE social media strategy at the RESOURCES tab on LyricMarketing.com and put an end to wasted time!

LYRIC'S MARKETING TIP #10:
BUILD A DATABASE OF CUSTOMERS

Is your database a coal mine or a GOLD MINE? A great marketing plan begins with a current and dynamic database. Don't be scared off by all the complicated database programs. Keep it simple, make a gold mine out of your contacts. Keep a master spreadsheet file (Excel, Numbers, etc.) that contains all the information on your clients, your prospects, target customers and friends.

Segment your contacts into the appropriate categories. Include first and last name, address, email, phone, etc., making sure that each field you include appears in its own column. Get into a good habit of putting all the people you meet and work with into this database, updating it on a regular basis. With this tool you can sort and select, copy and paste, upload into social media and email programs, and keep updated in order to maintain a thriving database. **Your database is your GOLD, lose everything else but if you have a current database you are back in business!**

LYRIC'S MARKETING TIP #11:
I CHOOSE YOU!

Provide information to your network that will compel them to CHOOSE your services over the competition. Think of the five areas that you are an expert in, then choose three topics for each and write a short post to push out to social media to engage conversation. Each post should contain content that answers questions and provides information that is educational to your clients and target customers. Creating and writing your own informative social media and blog posts will set you up as the knowledge expert in your field. ***When people need your service, you will come to mind!***

LYRIC'S MARKETING TIP #12:
THE HOLY TRINITY OF MARKETING

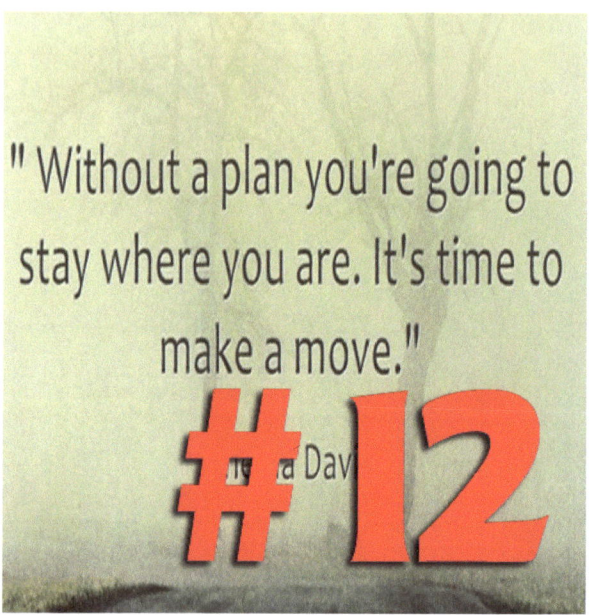

Any marketing initiative must begin with a well thought out plan and what I call the holy trinity of marketing: **assessment of your time, imagination and budget.**

#1: Be realistic about your time constraints and the amount of time you can commit for carrying out the marketing plan.

#2: Your marketing carries YOUR message, you are only limited by your imagination and the ideas and information you are able to produce.

#3: Money is a key factor, how much can you spend? Do you need to hire someone to help you? How much are you willing to invest in your future?

Begin your marketing plan with these three considerations, then set it into motion!

LYRIC'S MARKETING TIP #13:
DIVERSIFY YOUR MARKETING BASKET

In executing a marketing plan, it is important to be as diverse as the market you serve. Do not put all your eggs in one basket! Deliver your marketing message through a number of marketing vehicles: Social media, blogging, email, direct mail, sponsorships, and good old-fashioned phone calls that lead to one-on-one appointments over lunch or coffee. There is business waiting for you in all types of marketing.

Depending upon your target customer, you may want to focus on social networking to build relationships, or you may want to use the US Mail to deliver your message offering your services. You have to know your customer.

LYRIC'S MARKETING TIP #14:
THE SOUND OF YOUR MARKETING

We love what we do here at Lyric Marketing & Design, especially putting our resources to work for our clients. Our goal is to make your personal brand and your business shine brighter than the rest! We want to ask you this question: ***What does your marketing sound like?*** Is it a whisper that can faintly be distinguished against all the other noise? Or, is it a beautifully orchestrated sound that tells your compelling story?

LYRIC'S MARKETING TIP #15:
NEED A SURE DELIVERY?

Direct mail is alive and kicking. Despite a general attitude that using the US mail for marketing is from the dinosaur age, it is alive and well. Research shows that it evokes a deeper emotional response in the brain because it is tangible. Hummm, makes me think....when was the last time I received a great postcard that popped with information that wasn't just trying to sell me something?

Another good reason for using direct mail in your marketing is that it is guaranteed to be delivered. Electronic mail and social media is great and we can't live without it, but there are so many programs that have been created to PREVENT your message from being delivered. Take a look at your overall marketing plan, does it include some form of direct mail? Maybe it is time to plan a direct mail campaign that is designed to provide information relevant to your target customer, something they can keep and value. Perhaps a postcard that pops with great color and offers useful and valuable information, or maybe a follow-up handwritten letter to your client "A" list, just to stay in touch. There are endless ideas of how to use direct mail, so get outside the box and have fun with this one!

LYRIC'S MARKETING TIP #16:
VIDEO IS NOT JUST FOR MOVIES

Did you know that video is the fastest-growing digital content category? Here are some eye-opening stats:

- 70% of B2B content marketers use videos
- 58% of B2B marketers say it is the most effective content marketing tactic
- 85% of Internet Users watch online video and it's growing

Creating a video is not difficult. A decent camera or smart phone with a good video function, a compelling message, good light, and you, is all that's needed. I know I am over simplifying, but really, the time to create your video channel and post your own videos is NOW. Share content that is supportive of your business, information that is useful to your clients and target customers. Be generous with your information, but keep the videos under 3 minutes in length. ***What better way to tell your story and share your expertise?***

LYRIC'S MARKETING TIP #17:
DOUBLE YOUR PLEASURE

So many people ask me when I am in coaching sessions "*do I need another Facebook page just for my business*?" My answer always is "*no*". Today's transparent digital marketing is all about authenticity - being real - being you. What I suggest is to start with your personal profile and make it fun. Let it represent your personality and don't hold back on telling your friends what you do - just don't sell. Remember, social media is SOCIAL, keep it light and fun. When you get a large enough following and you have the time and resources to dedicate to building a dynamic Facebook Business Page, then go for it.

NOTE: Remember to keep your profiles complimentary to your business, i.e., if you are a nanny or a child care specialist, please don't post photos of you partying with the boys in your bikini!   XOXOXO

LYRIC'S MARKETING TIP #18:
YOU CREATE A BUZZ!

It's important to let your customers, clients, and the community see who you are as a *person*, beyond your brand. When I share photos of me on the jogging trail, pics of my "Friday-night-single-girl-grocery-cart", or rant about a common problem I see in the world, my networks support me with comments, laughs, or even disagreement (which can be good). Now that I have their attention I can begin to build a relationship that can ultimately lead to preference and action toward my brand and the services I offer.

Have fun with it. Don't be shy about sharing your knowledge this way - gone are the days of stiff-impersonal corporate advertising - open up your heart and share a little of who you are. People will see you as a unique individual who shares their hobbies, interests, and perspectives. People will buy from you again and again because something about your voice, your unique way, resonates with them.

LYRIC'S MARKETING TIP #19:
TOOT YOUR OWN HORN!

I know it's hard to talk about yourself, much less promote yourself! BUT in this world of social marketing, you must learn how to carry on a conversation, engage your clients and prospects with information that helps them know WHO you are and WHAT you do. It's impossible to do that without some blatant self-promotion! There is a difference in being "salesy" and promoting your business/service - a very fine line in fact. My rule of thumb when you do send out a promotional post, is to keep it real and in a conversational tone.

LYRIC'S MARKETING TIP #20:
FACEBOOK AD TARGETING

When setting up your Facebook ad campaign make sure your reach isn't too large. Focus your targeting on the right demographics to see better results. If your target is too large you risk getting lost in the crowd. Start by walking through the type of customer you want and where they are - i.e., Single female, age 25-55, interested in shoes that lives in your home town - drill down your demographics to identify and target your ads in this way and according to your brand message and ideal audience.

LYRIC'S MARKETING TIP #21:
IT'S ABOUT CONNECTING!

When you're scheduling your daily posts via HootSuite or the social media dashboard of your choice, don't forget that it is still about connecting. Don't get lost in the minutia of posting that you forget the most important aspect of social media, the people you are speaking to. The added help of automation and technology is great and we love it, just don't lose the human touch!

LYRIC'S MARKETING TIP #22: DELIGHT YOUR AUDIENCE

Step outside the status quo when speaking to your networks. Here are 10 great tips to delight your audience:

1. Be human.
2. Make them feel loved.
3. Capture their heart in the first 30 seconds.
4. Slow down and do it right.
5. Think integration and building a foundation.
6. Inspire them to be better.
7. Strike an emotional chord - make them feel something.
8. Focus on relationships and the heartbeat of social media.
9. Teach them. What knowledge can you share with them that will make them smarter?
10. Make it easy to engage with you. People want to connect.

The most important thing you can do to better delight everyone who comes in contact with your brand is to listen to them. Listen with a goal to understand. Don't just think about the next thing you can shout back at them, hear what THEY are saying. Bottom line, listen more than you talk. You'll be amazed how much you can learn about your audience when you shut up and listen. Try it!

LYRIC'S MARKETING TIP #23:
HOW VITAL IS SOCIAL MEDIA?

Social Media has taken on many forms over the last few years. From Facebook to Twitter, YouTube to Vine, WordPress to Tumblr, the list goes on and on and new networks are gaining popularity daily. We are consuming social media in bucket loads. It has changed the way we socialize and the way we conduct business.

Mashable.com posed the question, "What does social media mean to you?" As a business owner, it's important to know how my clients are participating on the social media platforms. So I'm asking you the same question. Take time and think about it, consult with a marketing professional on how to use social media, talk to young people about it. Get educated on social media's benefits and its liabilities, then you can make a decision on how to use it in your business marketing.

LYRIC'S MARKETING TIP #24:
WHAT'S WORKING?

Is your marketing strategy working in your favor? No doubt if you are promoting your business, you have invested your time and energy into multiple vehicles to spread the word about your services. The $64K question is "what is working"? This is where testing and measuring and paying attention to what you are doing becomes the driving force behind your success in marketing. Take a simple approach to get started. Write it down.

1. What are you doing?
2. What are the results you have seen?
3. Make a list of the marketing initiatives you have had over the last 12 months:
    - What did they cost?
    - What time was involved?
    - What results did you see?

This will help you eliminate wasteful and time consuming marketing. Be willing to change marketing habits that prove ineffective.

LYRIC'S MARKETING TIP #25:
CREATE AN EVENT - GIVE BACK!

Get in Front of Your Target Audience with an Event. Whether you are a sponsor at a charity event, or you are launching your own event to promote your services or cause, event marketing will get you in front of your target audience in a fresh and unique way. Imagine a room full of like minded people where you can present your business answer to their pain! Look for events in your industry where you could be a keynote speaker or sponsor providing materials, etc. Better yet, plan your own event around a charitable organization where you can rally the cause with your business voice to give back to the community. Invite your sphere of influence and keep the plans within your budget (it doesn't have to be huge), make it fun, have a party and people will talk and create the buzz!

LYRIC'S MARKETING TIP #26:
SILENCE IS NOT ALWAYS GOLDEN

You can't hide in today's tech savvy world. From YouTube to Facebook, Twitter to LinkedIn, your worst day can quickly turn into water cooler chatter to millions of users online. Whether an employee sheds some negative light on your brand or a well intended, "thought out" campaign turns sour, always remember one very important tip; engage, engage, engage!

When a large pizza chain tried to handle their recent PR snafu under the radar instead of addressing it directly with their customer base, they saw a temporary drop in quality and buzz ratings. The dreaded McDonald's Twitter campaign gone wrong was the result of vague hashtags and limited communication when the Twittersphere had a hay day with #MCDStories. So always remember one thing, when negative press is sprayed online about your company, face it head on, be honest with your customers. They're certainly talking with others about your brand. Hiding will only increase the chatter and decrease brand loyalty!

LYRIC'S MARKETING TIP #27:
ALWAYS BE TRACKING

It's easy to get caught up in all the social hubbub and overlook or minimize the most important aspect of marketing, tracking. There are hundreds of factors that come into play when measuring the success of an online campaign or website. So if you start to feel a bit overwhelmed focus on a few key metrics to get you started.

1. Time spent per page
2. Retweets
3. Un-follows and de-friends
4. Seven-day and 30-day active users
5. Exit page/last page visited
6. Human response lag

The Basics: page views, unique visitors, followers, fan counts, click-through rates, bounce rates, cart abandonment rates and load times are vital to tract so you can see the progress you are making in your online marketing efforts.

LYRIC'S MARKETING TIP #28:
DO SOMETHING GOOD

Putting good out in the world is a no-brainer, but have you ever thought about creating a marketing campaign around doing good? In today's social climate people are paying attention to what companies are doing and how they are giving back. In fact, the consumer will choose a product or service because of it! Add an element into your marketing that gives back to the community by supporting a charity or sponsoring a community program. Become the face and heart of your local area and build the love!

In a recent trip to NYC, the Lyric team was on our way back from lunch and ran into a beautiful window display that perfectly portrays today's tip. Designer Joan Hornig and Bergdorf Goodman had teamed up over the holidays to make philanthropy beautiful by donating 100% of the profits from the jewelry line to the charity of the customer's choice. "*It only takes one person to change the world*!" Visit her site at: http://www.joanhornig.com.

LYRIC'S MARKETING TIP #29:
YES! PRINT IS NOT DEAD!

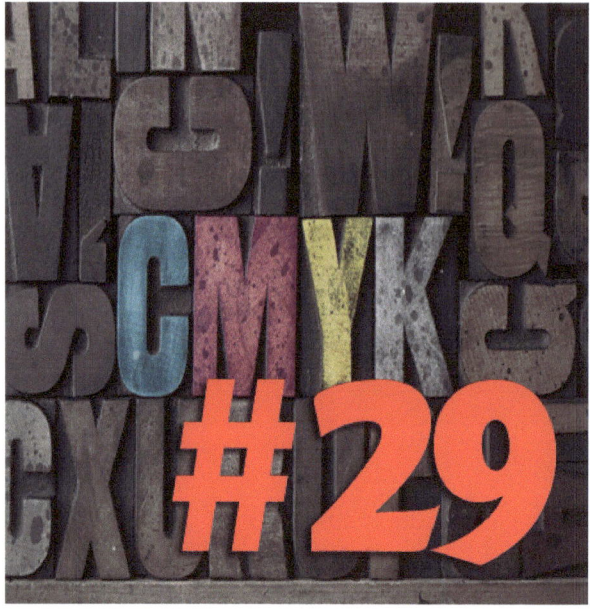

"*Print is dead, TV is dead, the Internet is dead*!" We've all heard these absurd accusations yet all three mediums are still alive and well. Print may be taking a hit as most advertisers and marketers turn to digital avenues to reach their customers, but print is stepping back into the spotlight and it just might be its time to shine.

As marketers, diversification is crucial when reaching our customer base. Now, I do agree that digital strategies should be a central focus in today's social world, but that doesn't mean you should overlook the power of print. **Here are eight reasons to rethink print:**

1. It grabs attention
2. It focuses on customer retention
3. There are no audience development costs
4. No reliance on advertisers
5. What's old is new again
6. It WILL be delivered
7. Print still excites people
8. Print lets people unplug

LYRIC'S MARKETING TIP #30:
FINDING YOUR BUSINESS NICHE

When you find AND connect with your niche you will develop raving fans and LOVING customer advocates.

If you are finding it difficult for people to respond to your generic offerings or messages, you would be smart to carefully consider how to find your special talent. It's not that hard, here are two simple ways to uncover your forte:

1. Look at your offering itself - your specialty, what you do best most likely appeals to a certain audience
2. Look at MORE than your target market - you have a specific industry you have worked with often where your product or service is needed, a group that is easy to target and has money to spend, they have a specific need and you have the answer!

There are other ways to niche, but this should get you thinking in the right direction. The bigger issue is **properly communicating the VALUE of what you offer**. If you help me connect with and find more clients as you promise, what will it really get me? More clients? More money? People don't buy communication skills - **they buy results.** As one of my favorite marketing guru's - Ali Brown - says, *"people don't buy a drill for the drill, they buy it for the hole that is the result"*.

So what is the result? Don't rely on your prospects to add it up in their heads. Don't rely ONLY on a "targeted" group. You have to *instantly* convey what you are offering and in a bold way and to the right people - people who understand, NEED, and will PAY for your services!

LYRIC'S MARKETING TIP #31:
A PICTURE'S WORTH

From Instagram to Pinterest we are obsessed with pictures. And now with the advancement of smartphone technology, it's easier than ever to capture your marketing right in the palm of your hand.

Pinterest is a great platform to showcase different sides of your brand. With multiple boards the creative opportunities are endless. For example, a real estate firm could use multiple boards to not only showcase properties, but stand out characteristics of the surrounding areas. If you have homes for sale in the downtown area you could create boards for favorite restaurants in the area or even an event board with pictures of activities.

Remember, a picture's worth a thousand words, so get creative! Even if you're not a photographer, smartphone technology lets us all take advantage of the countless marketing opportunities through images and social media.

LYRIC'S MARKETING TIP #32:
TIPS FROM RICHARD BRANSON

Virgin Founder Richard Branson knows a thing or two about social media: "I've built a strong online presence over the last few years and am always thinking of new ways to expand our reach. I think this is partly because I was already comfortable with the basic concepts: after all, my first successful business was in the media."

Considered "the World's top social CEO", Branson has executed a social strategy that brings a personality and authenticity to his online footprint both socially and professionally that is truly unique. So check out his top 3 tips for developing a powerful social strategy.

1. Social media isn't just a one-way street.
I always try to make time to reply to people. Many good ideas for future blogs are sparked by reading the comments online and the conversations they spark. If you're expecting people to be intrigued by what you and your business have to say, you have to genuinely be interested in their feedback.

2. Tell a few jokes.

As always: Don't take yourself too seriously. You have a lot of opportunities to make people smile via social media. When we started Student we were young and definitely just as focused on having a good time as on getting an issue out by deadline. For us there was no difference between work and play - and there still isn't today. Among my posts and tweets you'll find lots of funny tales, cheeky questions and the odd photo of me making a fool of myself.

3. Give them the genuine article.

Try to make sure your posts and tweets provide a true reflection of yourself, and not just your professional persona. Whether on social media, on a plane or in the office, you (and your business) are far more likely to make an impression if you let your real personality shine through.

Once you get started, you'll soon learn that by embracing social media you can keep in touch with and inform your customers to a greater degree than ever before. Through that exchange you will no doubt broaden your understanding of your business's horizons. So tweet "hello" and then publish a post introducing yourself and your company, because it's time to get the conversation started.

LYRIC'S MARKETING TIP #33:
SIMPLIFY YOUR MOBILE STRATEGY

After topping $10 billion in sales in the first half of 2013, new survey data from ComScore puts mobile commerce over $25 billion by the end of 2013. A mobile strategy can seem daunting to small and large companies alike but there's no denying the importance of incorporating mobility in your marketing plan. Whether you are a solo service provider or a retail store, you need to be accessible via mobile. Take a look at the list of actions below that you will need to use in building a dynamic mobile strategy:

1. **Assess your needs** - evaluate your operation and how you can integrate mobile effectively.
2. **Get clarity** - are you a service business, do you have a product? Who are you speaking to? What are the needs of your target audience and how can mobility speak to them?
3. **What are the drivers** of your business?
4. **What are the opportunities** in your market?

5. **Develop your approach**
6. **Direction Setting**
    a. Step 1 - Refine your Vision
    b. Step 2 - Ideation, Assessment, Visualization
    c. Step 3 - Roadmap & Next Steps

For more information on this subject, check out this slideshare by Propelics: http://www.slideshare.net/propelics/october2012webinarv3

LYRIC'S MARKETING TIP #34:
GREAT MARKETING LASTS FOREVER!

Great marketing will transcend time and trends. Whether you are using old school marketing like billboards or direct mail, if your message is skillfully crafted and your imagery pops, it will get the attention of your audience.

To create a classic marketing campaign, keep your message simple and stick to the authenticity of your story. Take your time to thoughtfully select classic imagery and honest messaging that tells your compelling story. If you adhere to these few simple techniques with the help of a professional marketing team, your marketing will continue to work for you for years to come.

LYRIC'S MARKETING TIP #35:
BE AN EXPERT IN YOUR FIELD

So you think you can do it all? So do I - well, at least that's what I USE TO THINK until I gained more experience and realized that honing in on what I do best and letting others do what they do best is the real secret to business success. And when it comes to marketing, focus on that ONE THING that you can claim to be an expert at.

Tell your story and market your expertise - be an expert on something. I believe the best success comes when you're focused on ONE THING that you do very well. Build your marketing and advertising strategy around that and you will build a name for yourself that will garner loyalty and trust for the service you offer.

Too many times in today's business environment we think that because we are CONNECTED that we can respond, perform, deliver, all the services that are now required - from technology to social media to business organization to PR strategies to everything. The truth is, you can't. So find your niche and stick with it. Become the subject matter expert in your field and show your target audience that you really know your stuff.

LYRIC'S MARKETING TIP #36:
SHOWCASE YOUR EXPERTISE

I want to tell you how you can develop an influential online voice. Build a solid content marketing strategy using information that sets yourself up as a thought leader/expert in your area and promote it with "push marketing".

There is a lot of buzz in the market today on content marketing. It can sound like a daunting subject to understand and take on, but it's really nothing new. We have always used this method in marketing, we are just PUSHING it out differently these days and have more places to share it. In short, content marketing is the focused distribution of **YOUR EXPERT** information to inform and educate your target audience.

Syndicating your content takes a well organized system, here is a short list of the key elements you will need to employ:

- **CONTENT** you write
- **PUSH** (share) out to social media and the web
- **MONITOR results**
- **ADJUST for relevancy as necessary**

Imagine a wheel like the photo here. Your content (information you create about your area of expertise) is the hub of the whole marketing wheel for your business. Each "spoke" supports the functioning of the wheel (the wheel MUST turn to get traction, right?) and the areas your message is reaching.

Before you jump in, you will want to start by writing a strategy that you can easily follow. Staying consistent and focused is one of the most important requirements in executing a content marketing program, so stay with it!

Related Tip:
Lyric's Marketing Tip #12: Marketing = Time+Imagination+Money
This tip has information that will be helpful to consider before you start any new marketing initiative.

LYRIC'S MARKETING TIP #37: CAPITALIZING ON 4TH QUARTER

During holidays and year end events, don't forget that your clients still need to hear from you. Don't slack up on your marketing during this busy time. When putting together your 4th Quarter marketing strategy, create your content to be relevant to the upcoming months - fall, football, changes in seasons/weather, holidays, gift buying, resolutions and new beginnings. Weave your story and present your services in a context that people will pay attention to and relate to in these busy months. And of course, make it FUN! Send out an eblast, promote a holiday offer on social media, run a contest drawing to grow your database via direct mail, throw a party, offer a discount on your product, give away tickets, promote a special gift item for your clients - the opportunities are endless. Now is the time to get your numbers up to start the new year with a bang - capitalize on 4th quarter with your marketing and you will be ahead of the game when the new year rolls in.

Related Tip:
Lyric's Marketing Tip #9: Save Time with a Social Media Strategy
    (check this out in relation to building your 4th quarter strategy)

LYRIC'S MARKETING TIP #38:
DON'T BE AN EGGHEAD!

This is such an important part of marketing - PLEASE don't be an egghead, use YOUR FACE in your marketing. With social media profiles being indexed by Google and used for marketing and online networking, it is important that you use a current image of yourself when setting up your online profiles.

In an article by Mashable "*This is why no one follows you on Twitter*", the writer explains how important your face is to your profile: "Users are seriously dissuaded to follow an account if they can't "see" the personality behind it. Don't leave your avatar as the default egg, an image of a celebrity or someone who isn't you, [and I would add even a logo] or anything too risqué."

The best social media "avatar" is a genuine pic of you and, considering how small the image is often displayed, preferably a head and shoulders shot. Remember: You can get more creative with your social media profile header photo and background. You are selling

YOUR services, YOUR story, so YOUR face is vital to properly represent your business. We use photos everywhere today to market and tell stories, from Facebook to Pinterest, so start with a CURRENT image of yourself, and don't forget to smile. If you haven't changed your profile photo in more than 3 years, it is probably time to do so.

Related Tips:
Lyric's Marketing Tip #8: Smile for the Camera
Lyric's Marketing Tip #31: A Picture Can Convey a Thousand Words

LYRIC'S MARKETING TIP #39:
SOME CLASSICS NEVER DIE

Simple sage advice: If it ain't broke don't fix it! I can't tell you how many times I have worked with clients that had a great marketing strategy in place - leads were coming in, sales were happening - but they got sidetracked with some new shiny object and stopped what they were doing to try "something new". NO! What happened is they lost time and money and wound up going back to a "version" of what they were doing before. I know it is easy in today's noisy marketing environment to be led off track and be tempted by the newest and the coolest gadget or program, but if your marketing strategy is working for you, why stop?

Those old classic marketing methods are tried and proven to work. If they are producing results for you, then by all means keep them in place. Don't ignore important "new school" elements you can employ to work along side them - metrics, more cost effective tools/materials, online syndication and videos to name a few. Old classics don't die out they just need tweaking from time to time.

LYRIC'S MARKETING TIP #40:
TAKE BABY STEPS TO YOUR GOALS

We all have big dreams for our business. To achieve the ultimate goal we must first know WHERE we are going and understand the steps along the way. For example, Sarah is a singer and her goal is to achieve success in the music industry with her songs. She must be familiar with the industry, know the players, what they expect and what they want to help move her along her chosen path. She is an expert at her craft, she knows her song and she can deliver it. Sarah's strategy would be to first produce a killer song, then record it, release it to the proper channels, market it accordingly to her network then reach outside her network to gain extended awareness and desire for the song. A photo shoot will be planned for the marketing of the song, then a video will be shot and marketed. **Baby steps.**

Each piece along the way builds a foundation for her following and brings her closer to a completed goal of a hit song in the market with the wrappings expected in the music industry - photos, video, performances and sales.

Don't let the long path to your desired goal scare you. It takes time, planning and execution. Focusing on baby steps will make the larger goal seem less daunting and easier to achieve. This is strategic planning and execution at it's best!

Related Tip:
Lyric's Marketing Tip #37: Capitalizing on the Fourth Quarter

LYRIC'S MARKETING TIP #41:
NO LONGER AN UGLY DUCKLING

Marketing is like getting a glamorous Chanel makeover. You've got it, I'm going to compare marketing to a great makeover. Here's my point:

A generic, mass sold makeup kit with white base, pink blush, and blue eye shadow is just about as effective as a mass marketed, genericized, marketing program. Over the last number of weeks, I have written about setting yourself up as an expert in your field and how to become a thought leader who provides information that your target audience not only wants to hear but needs to hear. From these articles I hope that you are beginning to understand the need for a diversified marketing strategy that hits some, if not all, of the marketing vehicles that are available to us [website, blog, social media, PR, email, broadcast media and even direct mail]. The next step toward accomplishing your marketing goal is to take these tools and put together a package that is tailored to fit you and your business.

Now, going back to my makeup example, I wouldn't sell you a kit of average makeup products anymore than I would suggest that you go to a generic marketing dashboard and spit out a bunch of drivel. You are unique, and just like your face and skin tone, your business and the way you provide your services are unique. Personal style has everything to do with how you conduct your business and represent yourself in your marketing. (Guys, I'm sorry for the makeup example, but I know you can get this too, you have been watching us put on our faces all your life!) So, the point here is simple: ***Find and engage your personal style and "apply" it to your marketing.***

Creating a content marketing program that compliments you and your services, that makes you stand out above the crowd, that wows people, that presents a look and design that is all yours, that is "applied" with precision and seamlessly delivered, has the potential to turn the ugly duckling into a graceful beautiful swan. Go for it!

Related Tip:
Lyric's Marketing Tip #36: Create a Content Marketing Program to Showcase Your Expertise

LYRIC'S MARKETING TIP #42:
WHO WILL YOU LISTEN TO?

This week's tip is to remind you to seek a professional marketer's opinion when you need help with your marketing. Take a few minutes to review the last five to six Lyric Marketing tips to refresh your mind on what I have been saying about creating your content strategy - now, take a look at what other industry experts are saying below about content marketing. Please note that I am not alone in my belief that great content marketing that speaks to your target audience is the key to your business success!

Here is what two key marketing leaders said at a recent Marketing Trends Conference on the subject:

<u>Forbes Magazine</u>: The Top 7 Online Marketing Trends That Will Dominate 2014 - by Jason DeMers

One of the main ways that companies are establishing authority and gaining trust with consumers is by consistently creating valuable content through a variety of channels. This typically involves relevant industry information that provides insight or entertainment to an audience. Doing so allows a company to steadily build rapport with its demographic and develop a loyal following. According to the Content Marketing Institute, the top B2B content marketing strategies are social media, articles on a business's website, eNewsletters, case studies, videos and articles on other websites.

By using one or more of these channels, businesses are able to build a positive reputation within their industry. This trend suggests that marketing to the masses through techniques like television ads and radio ads are becoming less effective. Instead, it's better to concentrate on inbound marketing, by producing valuable, engaging content designed for a specific audience.

<u>Suzanne Fanning</u>, President of WOMMA: "The Shifting Marketing Landscape"

The key characteristics that strong WOM (word of mouth) programs have: credibility, social component (an inherent hook that motivates consumers to share), repeatability (one hit wonders without lasting power fizzle too fast), measurability, and respectful (e.g., privacy). She also talked about the role that a good content strategy plays in the success of all types of social engagement.

LYRIC'S MARKETING TIP #43:
DON'T BE ANNOYING

You want to stay relevant, be noticed, and be consistent in your online advertising, but you don't want to be annoying! The most important marketing tip of the moment: when it comes to creating your social media ads (Facebook, Twitter and now Instagram) keep them in line with the network you are advertising on (this goes for your posts as well). There is such a fine line to this, so test, adjust, test and then adjust again! Social media ads are a necessary evil on free platforms like Facebook, Twitter and Instagram.

The key is creating an ad with a headline that POPS and draws in the social media user, yet blends in with the network personality. Make your ad relevant to the platform so that it speaks to that specific social media demographic. Also, remember that consumers are intelligent and already leery towards advertising on social media, so keep it light, fun, and stay away from blatantly salesy ads.

It's important to not that social media is a place where people meet to share opinions, experiences, meet old and make new friends, and generally communicate with others. If you want to be successful in social media advertising you are going to have to fit your message into the context and personality of the platform. It is different from placing an ad in the classified section of the newspaper, you will need to be more strategic about it. Use your social media ads to engage the consumer and tell them something important about your product or service and how it will benefit THEM.

Check out the article that ran recently regarding Instagram's first ad at http://mashable.com/2013/11/01/instagram-ads-first/.

Related Tip:
Lyric's Marketing Tip #32: 3 Social Media Tips from Richard Branson

LYRIC'S MARKETING TIP #44:
THINK LARGE

It's time to pull your head out of your tunnel vision and allow yourself to go where the sky is the limit. Think Large!

When planning for a new year or a new start, think: What did I do last year? Did I do the things I dreamed about doing? Did I take my business to the new level I had hoped for?

Your success depends on the marketing goals you establish and implement with a boldly crafted strategic marketing plan. Here are my **Five Out of the Box Marketing Ideas** for a sky is the limit strategic plan for your business - are you ready?

1. As an expert in your field, write an ebook from the content you have created this year and make it available on Amazon as an iBook, promote it on your website and over social media
2. Create a new video channel and videos that feature the content from your new iBook and promote it on Youtube, Vimeo and snippets on Instagram
3. Set up a weekly newsletter to blast out to your target audience with video snippets you have created at Animoto.com and a review of a chapter from your book - promote the links on social media
4. Throw several themed "Being Social" parties in a park and invite all the dog owners in your neighborhood to bring their dogs in costume (Easter, July 4th, Halloween, Christmas - according to the season) to celebrate the season and share the latest in dog news - promote your local food pantry and collect canned goods from the dog owners
5. Start speaking at the local Rotary and Chambers to share your expertise and make new contacts for business - talk about your dog parties and get a buzz going that will attract the media to your parties and eventually to your business

You may have heard of one or more of these five out of the box marketing ideas, and that's ok, great marketing ideas are usually right under our nose. It takes a well thought out strategy and a concentrated focus to make ideas like these work and be successful. Begin to plan now. THINK LARGE!

LYRIC'S MARKETING TIP #45:
FOCUS ON CHARITY GIVING

During the season of giving, have a holiday focus on charity by promoting your charity of choice.

During the holiday season there is a huge temptation to check out and leave your marketing on the shelf until the new year. Bad idea! Now is the time to not only ramp-up your PR and marketing, but to also have a good strategy prepared to kick off in January. Marketing for the last few weeks of the year when most people are focused on holiday and family, needs to take a different turn. I suggest that you have a holiday focus on your favorite charity. Take the focus off of you and instead spread the word to your networks about what your favorite charity is doing, their mission and their goals. Partner with your charity of choice to offer information via your public channels to bring awareness to their efforts and the people/goals they serve. This will hit people at the heart level which is what holiday giving is all about. Holiday marketing can be beneficial to your charity and to your business.

Here are a few ideas to have a holiday focus on charity giving by promoting your favorite charity:

› Post a link on social media of an interesting article about their services
› Post a photo of you or members of their local team in action
› Host a party in their honor and collect donations on their behalf
› Send a PR to the media about the party
› Donate a painting or piece of art in their honor and send out a PR
› Roll up your sleeves and go to work for them for a few hours a week
› Write an article about your experience with them and post online
› Gather testimonials from others who have benefited from their services
› Post a list of their needs and set up a donation station
› Help them market their upcoming events by posting their info on social media or printing their programs
› Send an email blast to your network with their link, say something good about your experience with them

The opportunities are nearly endless to what you can do to bring awareness to your sphere about your charity. And yes, it does take work, hard work, but the benefits will be great and think of the smiles you will be putting on those holiday faces!

Related Tips:
Lyric's Marketing Tip #4 – Do You Have a Compelling Story?
Lyric's Marketing Tip #9: Save Time with a Social Media Strategy

LYRIC'S MARKETING TIP #46:
IDEAS TO REVAMP YOUR BC'S

Unless you have updated your marketing in the last 12 months or so, my bet is that you might need to add a fresh look to your business cards. I am still a big believer in business cards (or calling cards), people keep them (especially if they look cool), and they will remember you each time they touch it. So make sure that your message and design makes an impact on that little 3.5 x 2 inch piece of real estate. Make it a habit to give every business prospect you meet your business card, and then some. Here are my suggestions for a kickin' business card:

- People love photos and love the human face, so use imagery - a photo of you, a great logo, or a themed image
- Use good card stock, no flimsy-flamsy paper, you want your card to hold up to the handling it will get
- Go outside the box, if you want to use a larger size or odd size for your business card, go ahead, there's no law against it
- Use great design and colors that pop

- Print on both sides of your card, take advantage of that extra space
- Don't put a lot of verbiage about your product or service on your business card, send them to your website for that
- Do not use a font size smaller than 10pt
- Include the information you want people to reach you with: Phone, email, Facebook and Twitter URL, address, and/or web address
- Add a memorable headline in a larger and bolder font
- Make it pop!

A fun example is my own business card were I incorporate multiple images. Each business card has a different photo but the same pertinent business/contact info appears on the reverse side. Since I am in marketing, I coordinated 5 different photographs to illustrate the many faces of marketing. My theme was fun, almost silly. Each of my cards carry a different photo of me (I used a total of 5 images) and the front of the card remains the same. For an extra pop, I designed a colorful custom QR Code that appears with my contact information.

You could have fun with this idea, regardless of what your business is, just think creatively. Here are a few ideas:

- If you are a realtor, use luxury home images for the different examples of architecture you specialize in
- if you are a jewelry designer, use photos of your most stunning designs
- if you are a consultant, use images representing the variety of industries you work with
- if you are a musician, use photos from various performances or playing different instruments
- if you are in business, use photos of happy client faces with their testimony of your amazing service!

There are many possibilities. Get creative and don't be afraid to get outside the standard old business card design. Do something fun that tells the story of your business/service passion. If you need help coming up with a new design, call on Lyric Marketing, we can help!

LYRIC'S MARKETING TIP #47:
A STRONGER PERSONAL CONNECTION

"Try a handwritten note as a way to say thank you to your client or prospective client, it is the best marketing investment you can make for the money"

I was in NYC recently and stopped at the Kiehl's flagship store at Union Square. I was immediately greeted and impressed by a young man who seemed to understand and know exactly what I needed for my skin. After a nice chat and very good retail experience he sent me on my way, but not before asking me to complete a card with my contact information so he could keep me informed of upcoming events and sales. One week later, after returning home, I received a beautiful handwritten, PERSONALIZED note from the same sales associate that had helped me. I was so impressed, and since I needed a certain lotion from Kiehl's, I picked up the phone and called him to place an order!

In a New York Times article "*A Stunning, New Social Media Tactic: Handwritten Notes*", MP Mueller wrote:

"Why is a 40-cent postcard so powerful? As technology races forward, people are increasingly starved for those high-touch extras, like homemade meals and personalized notes. Small businesses often operate at a disadvantage, but we certainly have the opportunity to establish the perception that we are more personable than our larger competitors."

It's an old-school practice - a handwritten, personalized note is a cost effective way to stay in front of your prospect and client. Don't send a generic message, that's nothing more than junk mail. Take the time to make it personal. Great marketing takes extra effort and will get you noticed, being personable and getting to know your customer is what will win their hearts.

LYRIC'S MARKETING TIP #48:
MAKE AN IMPRESSION WITH A POP-BY

There is no better time to do a pop-by to a client or prospect than now. There are plenty of opportunities to make an impression with a pop-by and work your database face to face. Make it fun and create a mood that is relaxed and festive when you are there.

If you are not familiar with what a "pop-by" is, it's simply when you drop in on a client or a prospect unexpected to say hello, drop a card or small gift, and leave. It's fun, it builds business relationships, and gives you the chance to greet your client or prospect face to face and even ask for referrals.

Pop-Bys will help you build a deeper relationship with people in your database and be a reminder of your services. While you are there you can get a pulse of what their needs and desires are so you can better serve them. Staying in front of your database is one of the most effective ways to build awareness and garner loyalty for your business.

Don't stay long, 10-15 minutes max. Bring a card or a small pop-by gift you can keep on hand in your car that bears your logo and contact information, and be sure to follow up with a personal handwritten note. The idea is to surprise and delight!

If you need ideas for memorable pop-by gifts, check out my friend Donna Bender's website at www.DonnaCo.com and browse through her inventory of fun and memorable marketing items you can leave behind. Get out there and have some fun with this one!

Related Tip:
Lyric's Marketing Tip #47 - Handwritten notes: An old-school practice that makes a stronger personal connection

LYRIC'S MARKETING TIP #49:
THE KEY TO SUCCESSFUL MARKETING

You Have To Write It Down!

There is something that happens in our brains when we write down an idea. It's almost as effective as speaking out what you want to do. When we add a written plan to a spoken idea, things happen!

To have successful marketing this year, you have to write it down. Create a written plan for your marketing activities so that you know what marking you will be engaging in, it's cost and time required, and when it will hit your market. Whether you do your own marketing or have someone do it for you, you need a written plan that is accessible. You should be able to analyze and review your marketing plan at any given time. A written marketing plan also needs to be kept current, an old, out of date written plan will not do you any good. So, if you want amazing marketing that is bringing you leads and sales, write it down. Build your marketing plan step by step with clear initiatives and follow up action items. *"If you build it they will come."*

Related Tips:
Lyric's Marketing Tip #12:
Marketing = Time Imagination and Money
Lyric's Marketing Tip #19:

Don't Be Afraid to Toot Your Own Horn
Lyric's Marketing Tip #30:
Niche, Niche, Niche = Customer Love!

LYRIC'S MARKETING TIP #50:
GET NOTICED ONLINE AND OFFLINE

Never make your customers or prospects work to recognize it's you in their mailbox or inbox. Keep your content fresh, but the look consistent on all of your communications – from letters to postcards to email blasts to web to Facebook posts – let your branded look speak for you!

- If you are sending postcards, make them POP with great content and colorful graphics and always "finish" them with your recognizable graphic logo.
- If you are posting an online blog, choose a great photo to illustrate your message and post it within your branded marketing look.
- Always finish each marketing piece with your branded graphic logo and contact information.

Keeping a consistent look in all of your marketing is what will "brand" your image and services into the minds of your target audience.

Related Tips:
Lyric's Marketing Tip #46 - Add a Fresh Look to Your Business Cards
Lyric's Marketing Tip #2 – Clean Up Those Nasty Marketing Habits!

LYRIC'S MARKETING TIP #51:
DON'T FRUSTRATE YOUR PROSPECTS!

Prospects want to reach you easily and they want to know that what you offer them is what they need. Make sure that the home page of your web site defines your product or service in a simple and understandable way. And most importantly, have your contact information clearly visible on your home page and at the footer or header of your website. **Don't Frustrate Your Prospects!** There is nothing more frustrating than looking for contact information on a website and not being able to find it, it's the quickest way to lose a potential client and BOUNCE them right off to the competition!

Here are two simple but very important projects to take on this weekend:

1. Make sure that your business/marketing message is clear on your website and tells exactly what service you offer
2. Display your contact information so that it is visible and easy to read – include your phone number and an email address

Related Tip:
Lyric's Marketing Tip #27: Key metrics you should always be tracking!

LYRIC'S MARKETING TIP #52:
FIVE KEY MARKETING METHODS

Don't Get Stuck In Just One Form Of Marketing

As you can tell from this year's marketing tips, I am not 100% techie and I am not 100% old-school. I firmly believe that great marketing is DIVERSIFIED. Look at your target audience as a passing parade. In order to get your message out more effectively, you need to catch them where they are. Sometimes that calls for technology, sometimes face-to-face meetings/networking, and sometimes it calls for old school methods like postcards, handwritten notes, and letters sent via US mail. So, my final tip #52 for you this year is for you to seriously look at your marketing plan and make sure it is diversified as your business moves forward.

Don't get stuck in just one form of marketing, make sure your marketing strategy includes the following top five marketing methods:

1. Emails
2. Social media
3. Pop-bys or one-on-one meetings with your clients/prospects
4. Postcards, letters and handwritten notes
5. A newsletter or industry specific blog post

There are multiple ways to use these five simple marketing methods. If you will incorporate three to five of them into an overall killer content marketing campaign, you will get the attention of your target audience. When they are implemented into your overall marketing strategy, your message will find it's way to your prospects and you will be remembered and the product and services you offer will gain preference in your market.

* * * * *

Happy Marketing!

A final note...

I know that marketing can be daunting, and so easily left undone, so I invite you to call on the Lyric Marketing team to be your marketing partners. We will help develop your "sound" and deliver your story to the market. We will target your customers with the focused, expert content they need, delivered with our expertise in YOUR voice. Let us help you tell your compelling story, freeing up your time to focus on your business and services!

Let's get started designing your content marketing strategy today. You can reach me personally at sandy@lyricmarketing.com or at 214-208-3987.

Love & Hugs,
Sandy

ABOUT THE AUTHOR

Sandy Hibbard is CEO and Creative Director for Lyric Marketing & Design, a marketing and PR company in the Dallas/Fort Worth area. After 15 years in corporate marketing and communications, Sandy Hibbard began writing feature stories for several magazines in Dallas, Texas. What started out as a creative writing outlet turned out to be a journey into marketing and branding that has given Sandy and her Lyric Marketing team the opportunity to work with some of the top business and entertainment talent in the United States. After 13 years, Sandy continues to run and lead her team at Lyric Marketing & Design in Plano, Texas.

Sandy has brought leading edge marketing, branding, PR, publishing and coaching to her clients. She offers the "whole package" - a unique blend of creativity and business acumen. Sandy's focus on content marketing is right in step with what is happening in the  industry today. She directs her campaigns – offline and online - with a passion toward developing the relationship with the client or prospect. She writes in a conversational and sometimes humorous tone that is open and honest and informative.

"Connectivity, systems, and great marketing are all pieces of the puzzle that an entrepreneur and business owner MUST have in place, but it is the people, and developing an authentic relationship with them, that completes the picture and sustains a successful business".

Highlights of Sandy's work include:

- Creator of "Lyric's Marketing Tips" nationally syndicated marketing column at www.LyricMarketingTips.com
- Author of the book "52 KILLER Marketing Tips" - 52 weeks of marketing tips available via www.LyricMarketing.com, book and ebook for Kindle available on Amazon.com
- Creator of the "Real Estate 411" information campaign and the Marketing Round Table for Realtors
- Creator of Saturdaysoul.com blog where Sandy writes on love and life and matters of the soul
- Author of the book "Heart, Mind, Spirit - My Second Coming" Poetry and Prose due out 2014
- Creator of "The HOT Top 10 list for DFW" - a monthly newsletter that outlines the "don't miss" events in the Dallas area.

Sandy is sought after for her expertise as a digital, content and social media marketer, marketing strategist, and blogger. She is known for her online contributions via the Lyric Marketing Blog, DTG Publishing Magazine, and her intensely personal Saturday SOUL blog. Sandy is an avid traveler and photographer and in her spare time loves to sing - performing jazz, blues, R&B, and soul standards, and gospel.

www.ingramcontent.com/pod-product-compliance
Lightning Source LLC
Chambersburg PA
CBHW040905180526
45159CB00010BA/2936